STANDARD 10-NOTE K

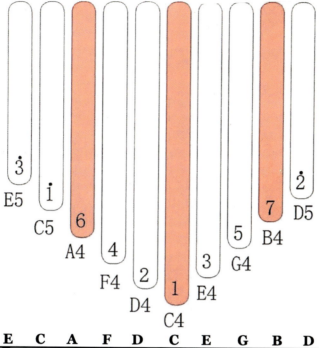

On most 8-10-tine kalimbas, the center tine will be a C note.

STANDARD 17-NOTE KALIMBA IN C SCALE

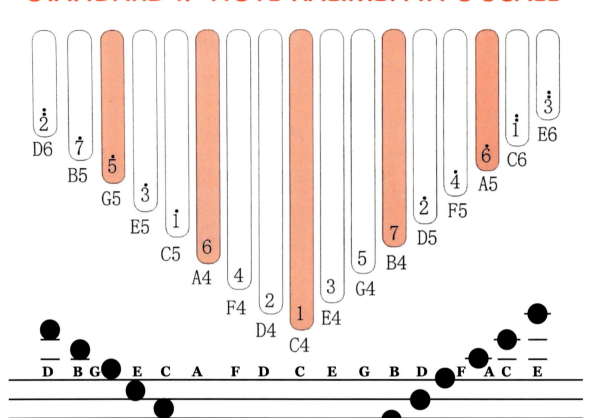

TUNING

If you want good sound, you must tune the keys. You can either use an entity tuner, or you can download a tuner app from your mobile phone. Android System app: gstrings, VITALtuner, Cleartune, and iStrobosoft.

Note: Sometimes the tuner is not sensitive to the keys in the high-pitched position. There may be resonance when you first start playing. Press the keys nearby softly, and then tune your kalimba.

BUZZING SOUND

Occasionally, the keys make a slightly buzzing noise. If this happens, simply move the keys left and right softly. If this doesn't work, just place a paper card between the key and the bridge to solve the problem.

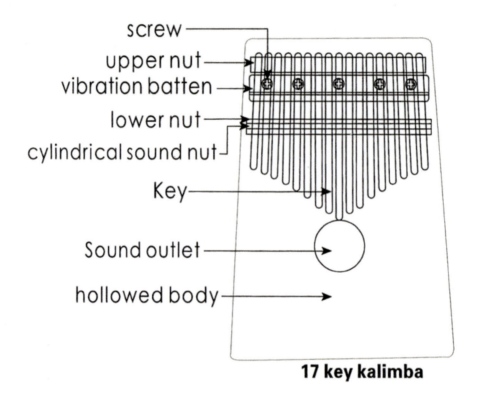

17 key kalimba

CARE FOR YOUR KALIMBA

When not playing the kalimba, please store it in the bag. Please keep your kalimba at a relative humidity level of between 30 to 60 percent. If the kalimba gets damp, rust can cause problems with the resonance of the keys.

HOW TO HOLD AND PLAY YOUR KALIMBA

- Hold the kalimba with your your thumb on the keys and your other fingers on the side.
- Using your nails to strike the keys will minimize finger pain and make the sound more crisp.
- Use your middle finger to cover the hole on the back to create a WAH sound.
- Train your thumb to move easily between all the keys on each side.

NOTES AND STICKERS

It will be useful if the keys of your instrument have letter notations on the keys.
Usually, these stickers are sold together with the kalimba, if not, you just need to get and apply any stickers with the letters.

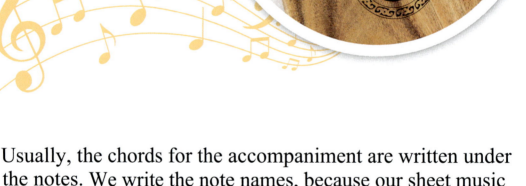

Usually, the chords for the accompaniment are written under the notes. We write the note names, because our sheet music is aimed for very beginners.

KtabS is a music notation system which was written especially for the kalimba. You can find this in most places and this notation can easily be read. However, we suggest that the easiest way to begin is to play with the letter notes in our book.

Each tab should match the number of tines on your kalimba. For example, if your kalimba has 8 tines, you need to search for "8-note kalimba tabs."

Our sheet music is not for a specific kalimba, but it is universal and suitable for 8-17 note kalimbas.

The low notes are usually in the center of a kalimba. The notes become higher as you move away from the center. The order of the notes alternate from right to left, going outward as you move up the scale. Taking "Do Re Mi Fa So La Ti Do", "Do" is on the right side, and then you will find "Re" on the left.

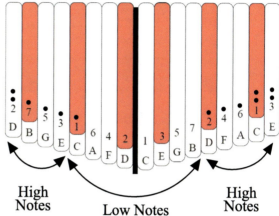

Also, the modern kalimba usually has enlarged letters representing the name of the notes. Often under the enlarged letter (or above the numbers), you can find one or two dots. These dots indicate the octave. Most kalimbas usually involve fourth, fifth and sixth octaves, and therefore can produce a high sound.

The central (the fourth normally) octave has no dots under the letters, the second (in reality fifth) is represented by one dot, and the third (sixth) has 2 dots under the letters. We also put one or two dots under the letters in the sheet music if they use an octave other than the main kalimba octave. The dots will help you to begin to play immediately.

Follow the letters… and begin to play! Usually the kalimba is considered an adult instrument, but with our visual, your kids will easily begin to play as well. Even if you or your kids don't know musical notes, you will confidently be able to play easily using the letter notation! This book might include only letters and it will be enough to begin to play, but we decided to add classic note symbols to help teach them and show musical notation.

If you are an absolute newcomer, our pictured illustration about musical notation symbols at the end of the book will help you.

Contents

Introduction

Part 1 1

Skip, Skip, Skip to My Lou 2

Humpty Dumpty 3

My Hat 4

I like to Eat (Apples and Bananas) 5

Cobbler, Mend My Shoe 6

Lost My Gold Ring 7

This Old Man 8

Baby Bumble Bee 9

The Bear Went Over the Mountain 10

Cherry Blossom 11

Ring Around the Rosie 12

Rain, Rain, Go Away 13

A Ram Sam Sam 14

Little Jack Horner 15

It's Raining 16

Au Clair de la Lune 17

Debka Hora 18

Part 2 19

Baa Baa Black Sheep 20

Twinkle, Twinkle, Little Star 21

Alphabet Song 22

Part 1

Follow the letter and music notes. Pay attention to the musical notation.

Skip, Skip, Skip to My Lou

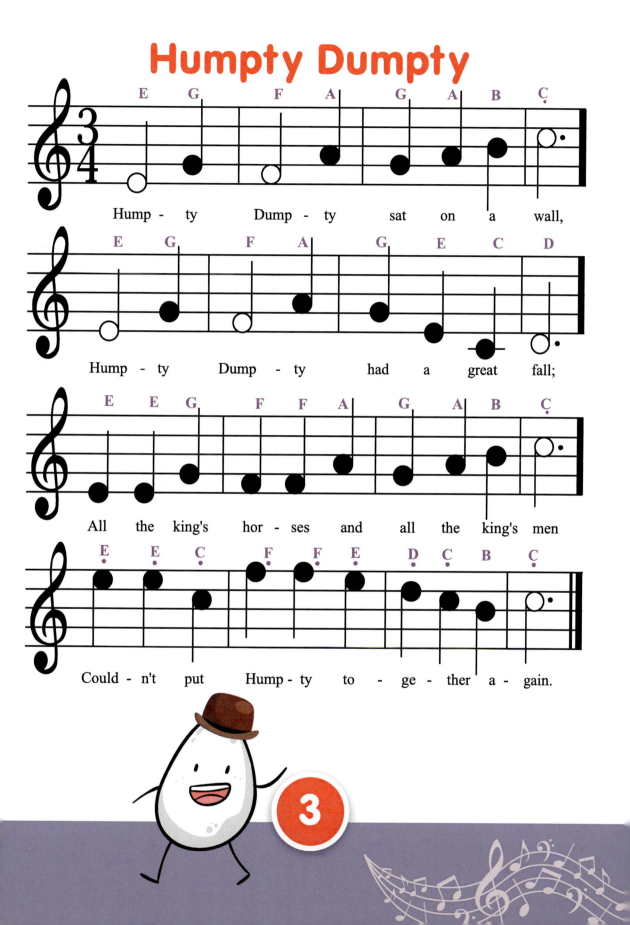

My Hat

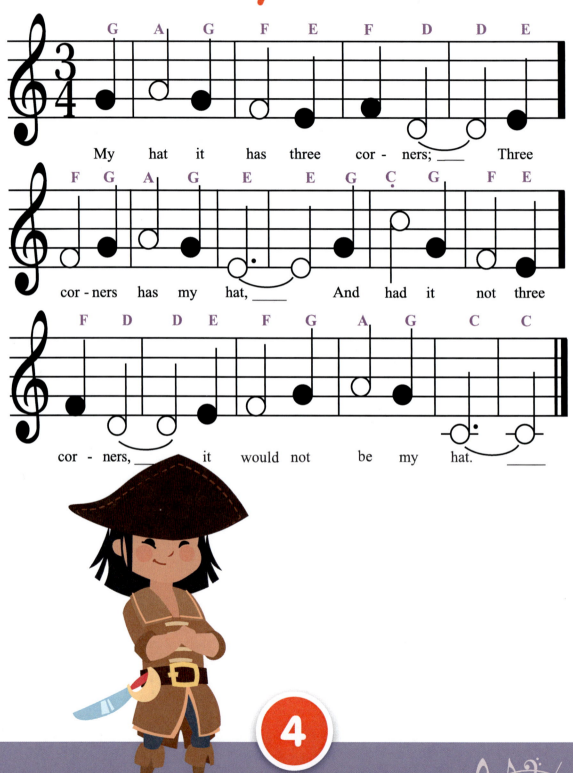

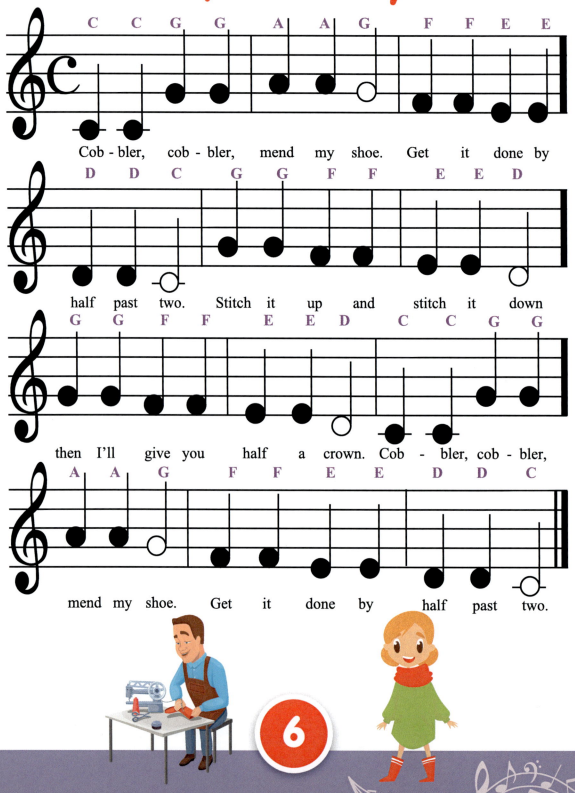

Jamaican folk song

Lost My Gold Ring

This Old Man

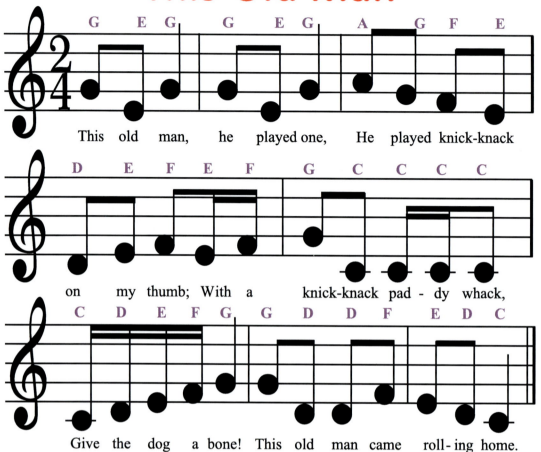

Baby Bumble Bee

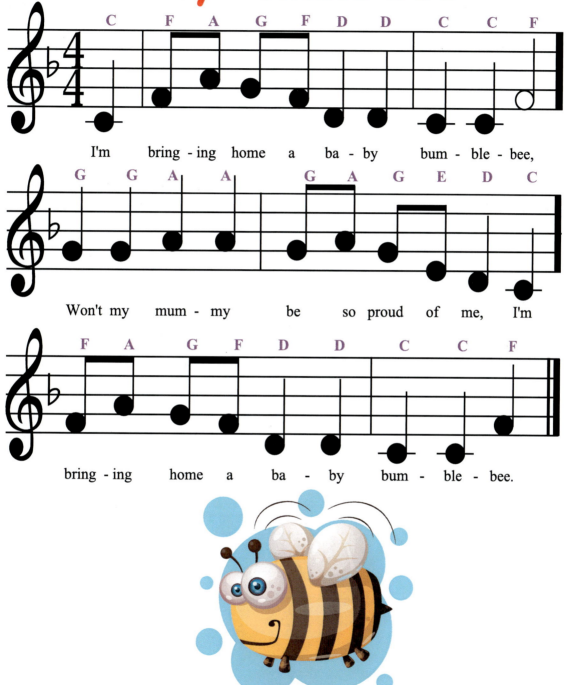

The Bear Went Over the Mountain

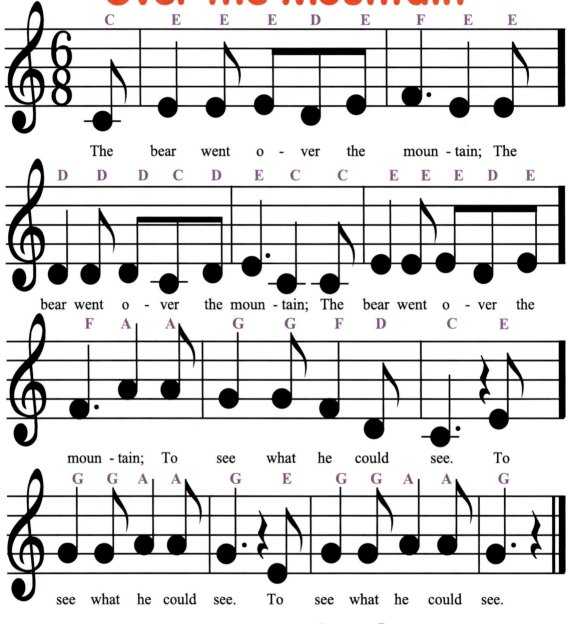

Ring Around the Rosie

Rain, Rain, Go Away

A Ram Sam Sam

Moroccan folk song

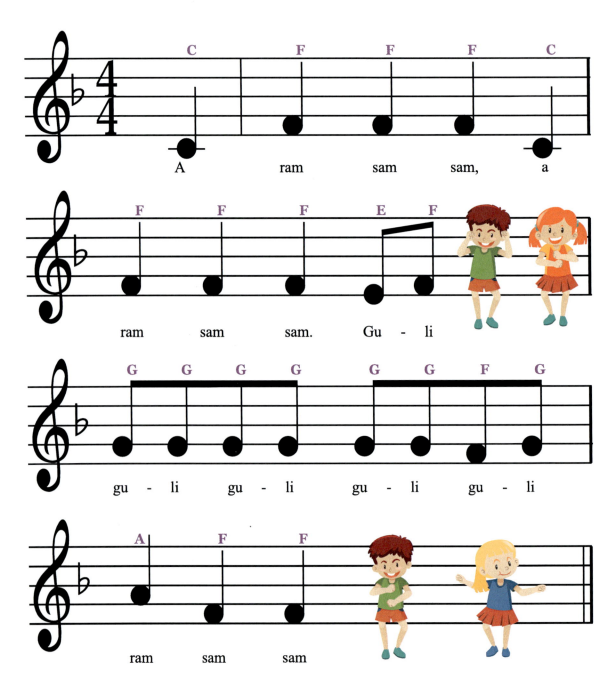

Little Jack Horner

It's Raining

Part 2

Here you will find 3 different songs with the same set of notes, but with different notations.
Have you ever noticed that Twinkle Twinkle Little Star, the Alphabet Song and Baa, Baa, Black Sheep have the same melody?
Yes, they are all based on a tune by Mozart, which is from a French tune, "Ah, vous dirai-je, maman" ("Ah! Would I tell you, mother?").
This is good material for understanding the importance of musical notations.

Baa Baa Black Sheep

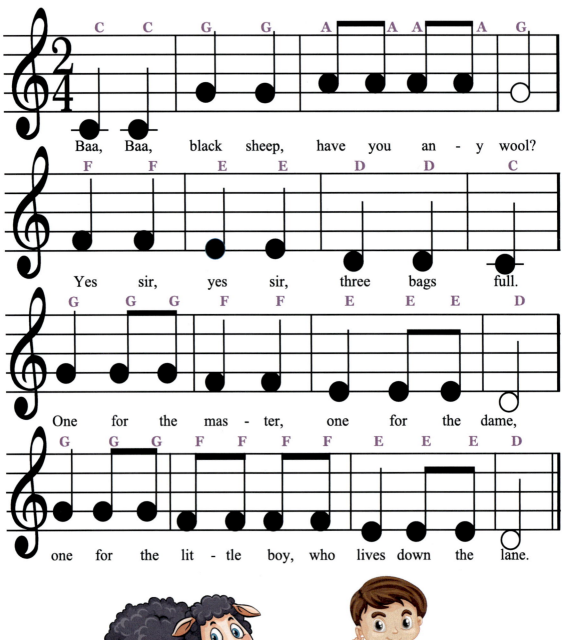

Twinkle, Twinkle, Little Star

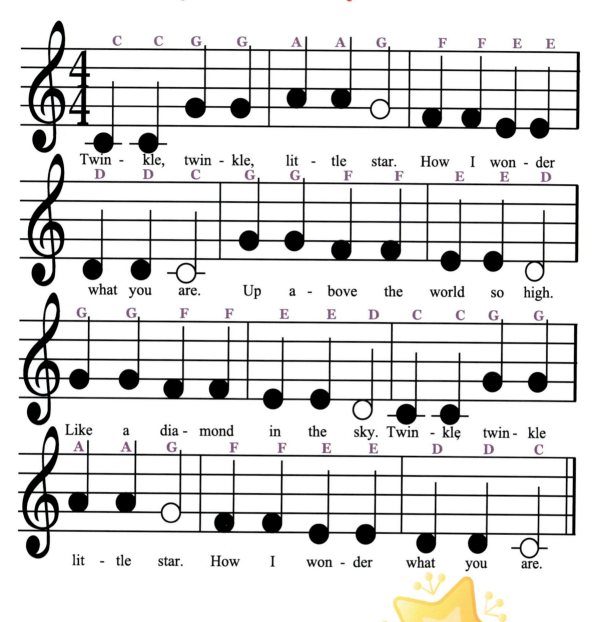

Alphabet Song

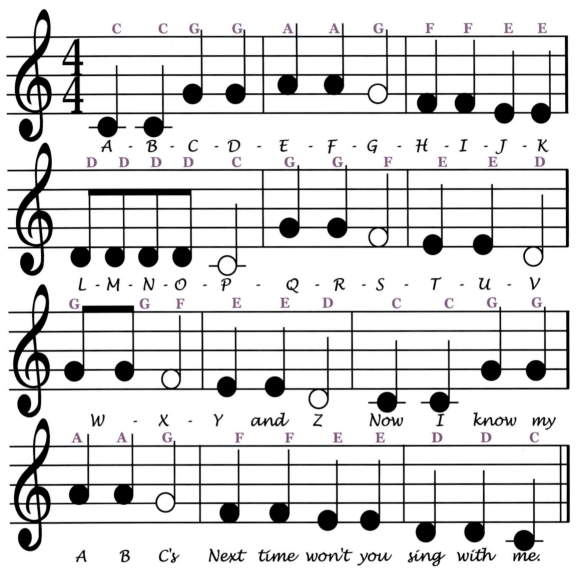
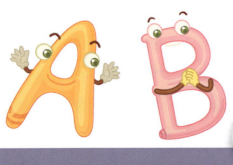

Music Note Values

How to Read Music

The empty HEAD

The full HEAD

The STEM is attached to the note head

The FLAG must always be on the right side

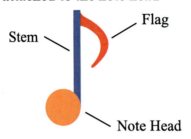

Stems may point up   **or down**

THE STAFF - The notes are named after the first seven letters of the alphabet (A to G). The name and pitch of the note is indicated by its position on five horizontal lines and spaces between.

5th LINE
4th LINE — 4th SPACE
3rd LINE — 3rd SPACE
2nd LINE — 2nd SPACE
1st LINE — 1st SPACE

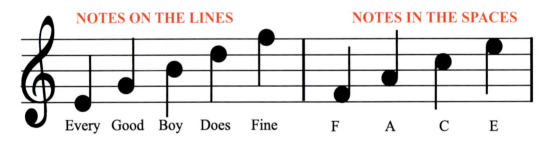

NOTES ON THE LINES — Every Good Boy Does Fine

NOTES IN THE SPACES — F A C E

TREBLE CLEF
The treble clef, also called the G clef, shows that the second line is the note G.

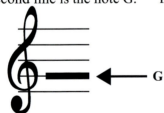

DOTTED NOTE
A dot indicates that the note should be held for an additional half of the note's beat.

TIE
A pair of tied notes indicates that the two beats are played as one extended note.

Bar

Bar (or measure)
A bar contains a specific number of beats within bar lines.

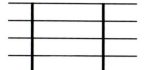

Double Bar
A double bar line shows the end of a piece of music.

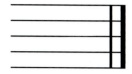

REPEAT SIGNS

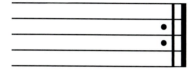

Go back to the beginning of the song and play again.

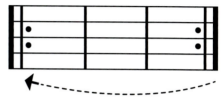

Go back to the "begin repeat" sign and play again.

Time Signature

Time signatures are used to specify how many beats are contained in each measure of music, and which note value is equivalent to one beat.

Number of beats per measure.

What type of note gets one beat.

4 = 4 beats per measure
4 = quarter note gets 1 beat

3 = 3 beats per measure
2 = half note gets 1 beat

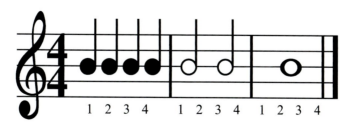

1 2 3 4   1 2 3 4   1 2 3 4

Made in the USA
Las Vegas, NV
30 August 2022